FORGIVENESS

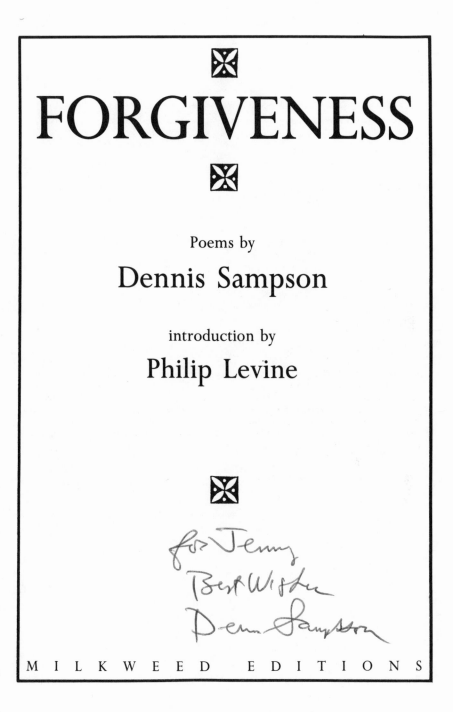

FORGIVENESS

Poems by

Dennis Sampson

introduction by

Philip Levine

for Jenny
Best Wishes
Dennis Sampson

MILKWEED EDITIONS

Acknowledgements

Some of the poems in this collection first appeared, at times in different versions, in *The American Scholar, Crazyhorse, The Hudson Review, The Ohio Review, Ploughshares, The Reaper,* and *Tar River Poetry.*

Printed in the United States of America
Published in 1990 by Milkweed Editions
Post Office Box 3226
Minneapolis, MN 55403
Books may be ordered from the above address

94 93 92 91 90   5 4 3 2 1

ISBN: 0-915943-50-6

Publication of this book is made possible in part by grant support from the Literature Program of the National Endowment for the Arts, the Arts Development Fund of United Arts, the Dayton Hudson Foundation for Dayton's and Target Stores, the First Bank Systems Foundation, the General Mills Foundation, Jerome Foundation, the Star-Tribune/Cowles Media Company, the Minnesota State Arts Board through an appropriation by the Minnesota Legislature, a McKnight Foundation Award administered by the Minnesota State Arts Board, the Northwest Area Foundation, and the support of generous individuals.

Library of Congress Cataloging-in-Publication Data

Sampson, Dennis.
    Forgiveness / by Dennis Sampson : introduction by Philip Levine.
      p. cm.
    ISBN 0-915943-50-6 : $8.95
    I. Title
PS3569.A46652F6   1990
811'.54–dc20
                                                                        90–41191
                                                                        CIP

for my mother and father

Introduction

Forgiveness by Dennis Sampson is that rare thing: a book of pain that in the end brings consolation. Its subject can be simply stated; it is about the lives we live, not the lives we hope to live nor pray to live, although there is both hope and prayer within these poems. It is also a book crowded with people, fathers, sons, mothers, daughters, sisters, wives, and almost all of them fail each other, and the fathers and sons seem to have an inexhaustible capacity to deny and defeat each other. Ah, you say, it is a book of daily living, a book of what is most common and despised. It is certainly that, but it is also much more. You might not think so if you read only these lines from "Touching The Outstretched Hand":

> Faith comes in the light
> and leaves with the light,
> the opposite of a lover.
> Little by little we learn
> to stop loving the world.

Before the poem is over it will have denied its own bold assertion regarding the meanness of our lives:

> Craning to see that flicker
> I followed with my hand
> above my eyes, she too
> loved that lightness in the poplar,
> saying, *Where's her mate?*
>
> This is where we live,
> tonight, like other nights
> rushing to embrace
> ones we love too much to have given up.

Could a book entitled *Forgiveness* not hold open the possibility that we are forgiven? Curiously, reading these poems, I find that a difficult question to answer. The title poem itself is a wonderfully full depiction of a small domestic schism. A father has come home drunk with a fistful of carnations to make up for forgetting "their dinner date and dance/at the VFW." The mother buys none of it. She knows she is entitled to her anger, and in the intensity of her grief she even lifts her arms "to a starless night,/ that she might be delivered from a sonofabitch." That settles it. The father flings away the posies and will not arbitrate. That night he even crawls into bed with his son, the speaker, who wants nothing but to be left alone. If it were not for the children's resourcefulness the next day, these parents might go on forever hoarding their righteous indignation, but the kids intercede at last and lead her to sit beside him on the davenport where "he gently touched her and they forgave . . . " Seeing this act of domestic contrition, the son derives a powerful lesson, which he shares with us, his readers:

> I realized that I could survive my father
> sleeping beside me through the night
> although I only wanted to be alone,
>
> seeing them together once again,
> my mother ashamed, my father blushing,
> having no other alternative but to embrace.

And indeed this book is that embrace, the son's embrace of this world in all its tragedy and comedy. Clearly here is the depiction of failure and forgiveness, so from what does my doubt arise? From the simple fact that Sampson's vision of our natures is so intense and total, so full of acceptance of our humanity that I seriously doubt he believes we require forgiveness for the manner in which the world has failed us.

If I had to characterize these poems with a single word that word would be "unblinking." The perceptions of daily living are so full and particular that I never doubt them, and by some miracle of language perfectly used they seem to pass directly from the imagination and memory of the poet to the mind of the reader. This is the book's artistry, an artistry so mature it need never call attention to itself. In the manner of Frost or Edward Thomas, Sampson's poems seem to be merely talking, one adult addressing other adults. Don't be fooled, for these poems are exquisitely sculptured and cadenced. In the poem "1959" a scene from the past is imagined with such incredible precision that it is fixed indelibly in all its sadness and glory. The speaker recalls being driven at night by his parents:

> Around the profile of my mother's cheek
> the dial light shines.

> She brings
> her hand, hung over the seat,
> along the neck of my father,
> then lays her palm open on his shoulder.
> The road rushes under us,
> leaving my mother inclining.

The movement is so delicate and right that the emotions are totally captured. This is free verse at its best.

While it's true that these poems can be tough–tough not in the sense of some young man's posturing but in their refusal not to see the world as it is, a world in which a son knows he cannot protect his father from the ravages of death and a father knows he cannot insure that his son will not become a killer–they can also be extraordinarily optimistic. "What's glory," asks one poem, "but a chance/ to redeem yourself for fumbling/ something in a former life?" In this world or in another like it, Sampson believes in the unthinkable generosity that creation offers us a second chance. Having read in the newspapers of a mother who tried to kill herself with lye because she failed to save the life of her child, a father goes into the bathroom and finds his son floating in the tub, asleep and well. Though he knows this is the world in which a "loving mother/ comes to grief/ below what Shakespeare called *deaf heaven/* and dies . . . hating the God that made her," he will take up his son in a towel, dry his hair, and send him "off to bed without a kiss." However briefly, father and son endure. That is the strength of these poems: they and their subjects endure.

> I say *Take heart*,
> even in
> so strange a place as this.
> I keep
> my vigil and refuse to move.

In an era of handsomely written books of poetry largely about their own skill with language, it's more than a little breathtaking to encounter a poet who writes for the most basic reason: because he has to. That emotional and psychic pressure that derives from the absolute need to write is almost everywhere in this book, and it gives the poems at times an almost unbearable urgency–they simply have to exist as they are, their stories must be told. "Why should there be anything other than nothing?" one poem asks, and it goes on to answer its own question as best it can:

> In the blue dawn in the cold,
> the souls of the unborn rise.
> This is not a vision.
> Folding my hands, I find I have been speaking
> to myself. The souls
> of the unborn know what I say.
> They have already heard this story,
> secrets I keep from myself
> I can't stop telling others.

This book believes in the usefulness of poetry as few books do; it dares even to believe that without poetry our lives would be impoverished beyond our own understanding of impoverishment, in fact they might not even be. In Sampson's poem "The Commandment" (one of the most amazing poems I've read in years), a poet recalls his own egotism of a decade earlier that allowed him to believe "the imagination placed/ me above blame and bitterness borne of living . . . " and he does not cry *mea culpa*. In his imagination he sees "the nightmare again"–a suicide he did nothing to prevent–and believes "everything/ is possible, self-sacrifice and brotherly love and death/ with more dignity . . . " A wise poem, it knows the limits of the power of the word, the limits of poetry itself.

> I cannot bring you back yet resurrect you
>
> in memory passing the paper mill tonight,
> maybe to explain why the imagination
>
> lies dormant until the fear of death comes clear
> to the human being, or until the love of one
>
> becomes the love of others so completely
> we forget why we were ever enamoured of ourselves.

To a hopeless world, Sampson has written a book of hope.

–Philip Levine

FORGIVENESS

III

IV

*We know that we will die, but we don't know
whether it will be today.*

—Cicero

I Wish I Knew Another Name for God

I wanted to speak
about the spider
between the daffodil
and day-lily,

not the black widow,
not the daddy long-leg,
but that fat garden spider
stopped between flowers,

a spider
speckled white,
big enough to eat a luna moth.

I wanted to speak
about the spider,
seeing the blue-bonnet wasps
copulating on the screened-
in porch,
bringing my eyes
so close
it must have seemed indecent
to the god of wasps

and all other gods

the god of spiders
the god of gravel
the god of wind-blown trash.

I

Making A Graveyard

They were making a graveyard. First, they took hold of the earth
  with those huge yellow caterpillars I was afraid of

when I was a child. They groped, and shoved the deep black loam

while the men in white hardhats stood and talked under the only shade
  tree there was for miles. At noon, the drivers climbed down

out of the cabs and sat next to each other, the wisps of cellophane

  blown up into the air and the thermos bottles shooting

  a glimmer of light
  just as they were hit by the sun. They looked ill-at-ease,

getting up to piss or just mopping their brows, cracking jokes about
  somebody else's girlfriend. I knew I could never go back to that
even if I had to. They broke up right on time, although one

lay face down in the dirt, asleep, until he heard
  the desolate engines start up and he got up and went back to work

like the others. They heaped the boulders off to one side,

then flattened the earth, running for cover before the thunderstorms
  broke, grasping their caps, while the wind picked up enough to rattle

the plywood shelter they had built for themselves. Pretty soon

  the graveyard took shape,

  you could divine it. No lumber anywhere,
  no forklifts, and the swaggering workers staying longer each day

taking fewer breaks. They brought in trees, evergreens I think,
  to get a jump on the headstones. Done,

    it looked like an island,
    fastidiously designed, with a picket fence

and a caretaker, wavering in the haze, who clipped
  the hedge and never looked at his watch, sitting up

in his pick-up while the ministers shouted their prayers. The funerals,
one right after the other, were beautiful to behold,
  especially when the casket, quivering with new snow,

made its way painstakingly over the graveyard grass.

    The gravestones grew in great number. By the time
    it was spring
    the marquee with special rates appeared

    beside the highway,
    "We deal intelligently with the dead."

And I had to ask
why I had come to love the sight of so many gravestones
and not be haunted by the mourners

laying down bouquets and wreaths on the graves.
Can you see a child buried and ever forget it?

In June, the caretaker comes and goes through the wrought-iron gate.
The sprinkler whirls.

Parents Gone, We Have to Stay with the Neighbors

I wanted to get away

so I climbed
to the top of the cottonwood
and stayed

twilight never so beautiful

at that height
while my sister sought me
in the garage behind the lilacs

singing *Dennis*

if you don't come out
I'll kill you
Are you there? Where are you?

I bore my silence like a saint

since I liked houselights coming on
for miles around,
hated my strange neighbors

stalking me

deep into the evening
with flashlights,
flinging their beams

against the poplar trees

Nobody thought to look
up at the boy
terrified of heights

in his pinnacle of leaves

peering down
until Karen screamed,
craning to see high in the tree

Encouraged by the cries

she
threatened to thrust me out
With an angry foot

I fought her

but couldn't shake
her loose,
almost losing my balance

Okay, I said, shouting

*I'll come down
if you promise not to hit me*
Confiding her dislike

of lasagna and vichyssoise

and creepy Mrs. Besselever
she agreed,
so slowly we descended,

our neighbors waiting

hands on hips
simmering in silence
Fool, she said,

you could have killed me

Hitting the ground
without a sound,
we turned to face our accusers.

Forgiveness

My father came home drunk and was dazed
by my mother's rage in the driveway,
driven back into shadows by her hand

while all the neighbors slowly turned
to their mowers in the dusk and their garages
shedding light on the lawns still spinning with sprinklers.

I had never seen him so quiet before,
holding carnations in his fist
as she answered her own questions and called

him inconsiderate for coming home so late,
forgetting their dinner date and dance
at the VFW. And when I thought

she had finally stopped, striding toward the door,
I saw her make the mistake
of praying, arms uplifted to a starless night,

that she be delivered from a sonofabitch.
He turned, no longer apologetic,
flinging the bouquet straight in the air.

They did not live together after that
for nearly a day, deliberately alone
in the farthest corner of the house,

my sisters and I conspiring to bring them together.
That night, alone in my own room, half asleep,
the full moon looming in my window,

I felt the hallway light on my face
when my father opened the door
and opened my eyes, seeing him strip to his underwear

and get in bed, saying *Give me some of the covers.*
I could have begged him to go away
and let me sleep, needling him

until he mumbled for me to shut up
but I stuck it out. When I woke
his side of the bed was empty, the blanket

whipped back, for he had gotten up in the dawn.
I lay there in the light, awhile serene,
then sat beside him on the davenport

while he moped, not looking at my mother
singing vindictively at the sink
with suds up to her elbow.

Taking my mother's damp hand
and leading her to the figure just as dazed
as when she raved in his face the night before,

my sisters on the other side, insistent,
forcing her to sit in silence beside him
until he gently touched her and they forgave,

I realized that I could survive my father
sleeping beside me through the night
although I only wanted to be left alone,

seeing them together once again,
my mother ashamed, my father blushing,
having no other alternative but to embrace.

.22

You took the .22 out of your father's closet
one morning to polish the barrel with a cloth,
first the inside, glittering when you gazed
down the long eye held up to a window,
then the dark-brown stock, nicked and scratched,
that loved the pressure of your cheek when you brought
a magpie down in the grove above your house,
a flutter of black wings collapsing through
branches without a sound. From a clump of
strawberry blossoms, the scared eye stared back
at you and you left it there, too afraid
to put it out of its misery.

Laid out on the table, shining, the .22
had a curious beauty. It tempted you,
although you knew it was empty.
You checked the chamber again and again
before squeezing the trigger, then put it back
in the closet with your father's suits
and wing-tipped shoes, where it remains,
unused for two decades by either of you.

If you went back to that house you would find it
fallen along the wall, the bolt swung open
and chamber caked with dust, and copper bullets
scattered in a small wooden box in the basement,
with antiquated keys and nickels and pennies.
In privacy you would do it all over,
polishing the barrel with the soft cloth
and placing the .22 on the table
where it would wait for you,
as if ablaze,
like one of the dead present and burning everywhere
and all at once in the mind of a child
ready to be lifted up out of his grave at last.

The Door that Only Opens on Its Own

When I consider your heaven, the moon and stars
come out together in the winter sky,
the moon being slight, and I drag my sled
back from the valley whirling with new snow,
touch my cheeks: no feeling. All of the houses
shed their yellow light across the white lawns,
a door opening billowing smoke and the dog
let out and in. And then I sense,
I think of the first time, a loneliness that won't
be compromised—clouds passing below the moon
and counted stars (three in the east), and wind so cold
it seems to realize a horror I can't divine.
Carrying my sled, nearly slipping twice,
I burst into the warmth and am welcomed home.

*

Closing the door to the closet my father stands
beside me and we wait for the click,
barely discernable unless we listen
closely, letting the benevolent spirit out
to hover ever so lightly from living room to kitchen,
where my mother plunges her hands
in dishwater and light from the backyard brightens,
where Linda, her palm against the glass,
leaves a momentary print then presses
that hand to her face, opening her mouth—
a spirit inquisitive yet willing to remain
days inside the closet until the door
swings open and he's freed,
issuing from the darkness of coats and hats.

*

There is no help for him in God. My uncle rages,
daring in his drunkenness, from above,
tearing the calender down and thrusting
a finger at a date. *Don't ever forget
the day my child died*; and I am bending
just beyond the wall, Linda right behind me,
her hand on my back, whispering, *What's wrong.*
I see my aunt weep into her palms, my mother
striding between them to take that calendar
from his fist, which she places on the table
set for three. Having held her sister in her arms,
later she speaks on the porch above my window
to the man who has nothing to say. It's June.
A jar of crickets, captured last night, sings in the room.

*

On the night the aurora borealis shone
we all looked up and called our neighbors out,
wind at evening fading to a sensual flow
in the hissing tree between the house and street,
lasting long enough to be defined
as prayer, as patience, as the gentle placing
of hands on a child's head
who looks at light long after mother and father
begin their conversation in the dark. It blooms
then is borne away above the moving spruce,
returns, observed until the neck begins to stiffen.
Step back, and say aurora, another name for light.

*

Up late, looking at fireflies
I can't understand, I am strict
with my father running me down in the dark
after I slapped my sister in the face. He flung
me round and his hand rose and fell
until I cried no more. I walked away,

27

shaken, exiled to my room
by a man who would apologize to me soon.
Yet I see myself leaving,
returning with money enough to make him mad,
with many women, beautiful beyond despair.
The fireflies fade, all at the same moment,
turning the world to dark. To light.
And then my father sits with me and speaks.

*

He says the secret is death. And death is long
or weaves its way back into life again,
such as the transformation of the Cynthia moth
from grub to flight,
across the fragility of purple blossoms.
Where have you gone? Where will I look for you now?
And I will never know as well as I do now,
although the constellations would intrude
between the mind and God, that graven image
only a child could be frightened by
an hour or so, and then forget,
forgiven for his innocence, fast asleep.

*

Once I stubbed my toe on the bottom step.
I struck the wall, but kept my angry silence,
saving my words for God gazing down
at me – that physician who does not touch,
curing according to whim. I blamed Him.
That evening, unable to sleep, I weakened and began
to weep, oblivious to my mother
at the sink, drawing water for her Scotch.
"Are you asleep?" My silence surprised
and frightened even me. Groaning
toward the wall, I waited. She waited,
wondering what was wrong. I did not breathe.

*

Grouchy in church, impatient to get away
from the monotone of sorrow and warning
Beware, we shall all be judged, Linda kicking
her shoes above the polished hardwood and Karen
pretending a maturity she sees in my mother's face,
I cannot follow what is being preached. Instead,
I watch a spider riding a filament
visible in sunlight through painted windows,
hesitating just above the heads
cocked back to sing in chorus to their God.
It stops, precisely as their voices rise,
re-evaluates its task and then withdraws.

*

This is my flesh, my blood,
my mysterious spirit I will not call God,
rather a concern for Karen,
compassion understandable to the fly
frantic for a shadow to cross its path.
I put my mother in a room with light
to read the scripture written in her hand,
my father in a valley, swept by grass,
going away on a road that does not last
past the orchard, passionate as dawn.
Memory finds my sister's hand too
in the night. I take her hand,
having been told to do otherwise.

*

I played with the turtle that I caught,
a gangster, who will not confess,
struggling to make it to the swamp
before I scooped him, scored
with orange – an introvert by nature.

I held him out all the way home,
hiding to surprise my sisters—either one.
I put him in a shoe-box, but he escaped
that night. . . not with any assistance
from his kind. The turtle has learned
the language well enough to keep silent,
of all God's creatures the least likely
to be grateful for a death
delivering him into the face of a strange creator.

*

Where is that man, my father,
folding his hands at supper before the glass
is raised, and everyone rejoices
in a community of eaters reaching to take
hands under the table? He changed
in his sixties, became fastidious and deranged
with questions I had to answer several times;
a tiny man, whose slender hands
hardly could hold a glass.
I hear him now, playing the clarinet
perfected in a lifetime,
lifting the ultimate note above his head
and hovering there, embarrassed when I come into the room.

*

Tired of being alone
I walked into the prairie blossoms, praising Him
in a way I understand
only at a distance of twenty years,
the half moon, shining down on me,
beautifully detached—with night not far behind.
I waited for the word that would not come
in spite of my vigil,
a magpie reappearing above the nearest maple.
Made blameless, in my eyes,

I could feel the flow of eternity in my clothes,
blue and moving,
evident in the pressure against my face.

*

Behind every shadow crafted to evoke
the past, the killer lurks,
death the only lesson not learned from observance.
In summer my mother plucks the flowering cactus,
forcing it into the company of strangers,
a tulip, too heavy for its stem,
flop-eared iris, watching it wither
over the course of a year– two days human time. Upstairs,
I listen to my window hiss, wondering
why the day moon does not move,
although we move, under the only star for miles around.

*

The snake is able to live with its reputation,
a rivulet of flesh, hyperactive in the presence
of human feet–a fairweather enemy to the rat,
not to be trusted. Does it deceive
as we have imagined, its slither
making the lawn off-limits for a week? I learned
to look for the diamondback, coiled on a boulder,
when I entered the kingdom of the skunk and cow
just outside town, that unraveling lace
that reared its head one afternoon
and glanced back–too close to being human.
Hidden, until hungry, intransigent,
having forgotten the apple, it has to vanish.

*

Coming out of the bathroom, warm and wetness
still down my back, I catch my mother

dressing in the half-light beside the mirror,
bending to tighten her nylons streaked above the knees.
I don't believe I've seen her naked before
with these eyes—surprisingly beautiful to me.
And I remember hiding beneath Karen's bed
while she unveiled her nakedness to me,
running her palms over nipples hardening
to a point. She caught me once,
searching for something under the single bed.
I lied, and she believed my lie; she let me go.

*

Swimming in the river, or straddling my father's back,
my mother getting up to cup water slowly
over her shoulders and shouting not to splash
when we burst up from underneath and laugh,
we stay together. Then only Karen and I
are there, father wrapping Linda with a towel,
gasping for breath as we go underwater
far enough away so that
the current carries us, ecstatic,
laughing when our heads are lifted again,
fighting inland, freed, our faces red.

*

It was the wind where I was born,
speaking at evening and at dawn,
the rain across my palm
projected out the door while my father slept,
his back to the family; the flow
of light to dark and darkness endured in sleep,
a hawk progressing across the simple sky,
breathless and blazing as the face
we cannot look at, and live. I was struck
by the resemblance to my father,

only able to communicate with his eyes,
a reluctant look, laboring to get away.

*

If I sprawl on the sofa and suppose
the closet door that opens on its own
holds back the knowledge of another world,
would it click open when I count backward
more and more slowly to the nothingness
of a circle, a gradual shadow
cast by the dining-room light across my eyes?
Tonight I suddenly realize
enough to converse with the medium there.
We hardly ever speak and never meet,
not even now as I approach zero
and am faithless at the figure of a swan,
and am filled with faith when I start over again.

*

What happens to people in heaven when it thunders?
I hear my younger sister whisper after the blast
draws light from the church and changes
the aura around the altar candles,
a yellow glow that seems holy now
as I stand with my family and bask
in sudden darkness, the visiting priest quiet
and several parishioners hurrying
to find the fuse that completely ruined prayer.
What happens? Do they stumble
over each other till heaven is made right?
Such a surprising question out of the dark,
Linda's simplicity requiring an answer.

*

The final angle of light in my window,
filled with infinites, or just dust,
fades and graciously admits
nighttime in late July into my room,
a rapture, after the nap, that I abide
until the call to come up. For now,
lying on my side, I see the spirits rise,
a riddle I'm inclined to figure out
another time. I will pass my hand
through that,
never catching the specks,
resuming their ascent when I stand back.

Getting Fired

That night after getting fired I sat
in the living-room and waited for my father to get through

his disgust – pacing, pacing – waited for him to find his way

past accusations I was lazy and never lifted
a hand – a smartass

that lipped off and couldn't look adults in the eye –
waited for the shame

when something so delicate is touched
it will never be the same, like the baby

magpies I caressed high in a maple
only to learn later

their mothers hated the scent of human flesh . . .
waited for the pain we name fatherhood,

we name strength,
to dissipate and be replaced by grace

of a hand set down firmly on the upper bone of the shoulder,
that fellowship that comes of being enemies

and now friends . . .
and I waited for the silence after the ultimatum

so searing it made me wince,
when everything is reconstructed again.

When a father finds out a son is fired
on Friday because he did not understand

the difference between a plumb bob and a compass,
taking all the rage of a stranger

in the middle of a construction lot in May,
is not the father supposed to show mercy

and seek to console, opening his past
to an anecdote about his greatest humiliation,

a slap by somebody he loved
to tease, changing the way he looked at the pitiful?

But my father wanted me to fight back that night,
like a child

flailing in the midst of his torturers at recess,
wanted me to resolutely defend,

raising my face to his face without saying anything
and one of us backed down

and both of us were changed.
Trailing two daughters up the walk,

peace was restored by the appearance of an angel
the following day. I was ashamed

while my father had shown
the power of humility was immense when he stepped back,

silent beyond all saying.

Coming Home Late and Alone

That was the summer
my father had cancer and demanded to be left alone when he slept
and my mother strung a cord from solitude
to solitude, scolding us for making the slightest noise,
bursting into tears when we sassed her.

Crossing the kitchen floor
and opening the refrigerator brimming with shimmering light
I dared my mother to reproach me. "Is that you?" she asked.
"Yes," I said. "It is me." "It's midnight, Dennis.
You need to go to bed."

And so I slipped off my shoes and tiptoed
past my father's room and stopped as I saw him bent over
reeds to his clarinet, all neatly aligned on his bedspread.

I wanted to remember even the glow
around him, the delicacy
with which he fitted the finest reed into his mouthpiece.

Entering my room
without turning on my light, so that through my window
I could see the lovely cup of the moon going down
over Duncan's grove, I sat on my bed and saw my father

over a year ago,
lifting his clarinet above the heads of the orchestra,
holding the final note of the solo
until the trombone took over
and my father acknowledged the audience with a nod.

1959

My mother and father are
talking in low tones in the dark
of the front seat. I can see
stars streaking across the window.
No, not streaking . . . they are still.
The radio changes from song to talk
after I lie quietly for a long time
with my head on the white pillow.
They know I am awake, but our lives
are not the same at such
an age, so they don't care
if I listen to their wish
for a better life, the white-stone house
with many windows, worn by wind
and rain, another son,
concern for Uncle Harlan,
sick last winter, thinner and thinner
until the sickness lifted
like a veil and he came back to us.
They do not even
turn their heads, watching
that island of light before their eyes
pierced by a line that lasts always
as long as the night.
Around the profile of my mother's cheek
the dial light shines.
She brings
her hand, hung over the seat,
along the neck of my father,
then lays her palm open on his shoulder.
The road rushes under us,
leaving my mother inclining.
She is frail

in sleep
and lightly breathing,
belying the silence that survives
vivid as these lights
beamed to high
the instant I fall asleep.

II

Touching the Outstretched Hand

"Brother, the world is blind,
and surely you come from it,"
is what Alighieri wrote in the *Purgatorio*,
his vendetta of ice and fire
behind him and the winding climb
to Beatrice half over,
yet what lingers for me is not the aura of heaven
but the eagerness to speak
as easily as you or me
of the cathedral gleaming in the mist.
Whatever hope we had of joining that Florentine
is spoiled
when we look up and see the evening.
I would have let everybody out.

Faith comes in the light
and leaves with the light,
the opposite of a lover.
Little by little we learn
to stop loving the world.

Who is this?
Dante walking toward me
with his listening companion?
Don't they know
the cigarette one lifts to his lips
and throws across the asphalt
makes me wish
I were as certain of my purity?
Why do they linger? Why do they look so tired?

It is hard not to think
of a heaven for everyone tonight,
even the widow
at the heart of town

lighting fire to the azaleas
by her fence. Let a cry
go against sending her to hell.
Her Christ will come, before the end of the year.
The stars appear far away,
Venus evident above the maple
brightening this side of us
yet wider than the light
in Filippo Argenti's eyes when he tried to climb
out of the mind of Dante
during their descent from wail to wail.

I have thought about hell,
how it might be
with day and night on fire,
everyone
together
forever.
I prefer mystery above my head,
enough for the mind touching the outstretched
hand of Adam,
the fingertip of God.

And I remember the rage
on the widow's face
changing when I named
the warbler in mid-song.
Craning to see that flicker
I followed with my hand
above my eyes, she too
loved that lightness in the poplar,
saying, *Where's her mate?*

This is where we live,
tonight, like other nights
rushing to embrace
ones we love too much to have given up.

Elegy for John Berryman: An Atonement of Ordinary Flowers

Why not compose a prayer
even if this means acknowledging God,
an atonement of ordinary flowers
where, wind-driven, I agree to seek
the meaning of my being here?
Instead, I find,
noble as the rhodora in Emerson's poem,
the only
honeysuckle left of spring
outside my study—one yellow
and one white.
Truly I do not know
enough to speak
of solitary flowers and the like
or of the cardinal I saw today
crossing tree to tree
and singing. Ten years
ago I wrote about a field of wildflowers,
meadow-rose and daisy,
a scattering of blackbirds
trailing one another across the sky.
I carved my name
on stone, opened my arms—waiting for a sign.
I can't recall what happened
after that,
although I know a meadowlark appeared.
My litany
was equally
sublime, song of the meadowlark mimicked
to a 't'. Yet I
am thinking now of the rhodora, John,
which makes me see
the singularity of all flowers
blossoming alone—a focal point
the eye may be grateful for,

having followed that cardinal
from the mimosa
to the ash
and back again, a solitary flower
whose presence
amid the serenity of summer says *I am*.

Robert Lowell:
"In that season of joy . . . "

I missed your reading
but for a month devoured your sonnets
scouring the history of wife and child,
an almost
cheerless litany for the spirit
that would not die
as long as you kept on talking. By candle-light,
a night of wrath
that made your "watchmaker God" seem wrong,
waiting
for electricity to flood the page,
I looked hard
at the inhabitant of your castle
over the Atlantic,
kinsman to Roderick Usher
going up those stairs
with a woman on his mind.
Only your phantasms were contemporized.
What did I find?
Faith,
fueled by earth's finite horrors,
hell's perpetuity,
and yet you had no concept of heaven
you couldn't rebuke,
having never experienced it in life.
Is that why
you delighted in Brunetto Latini's flight
enough to find
your own words elbowing Alighieri aside?

Why are we so hard
on the voice that roared
in an undertone?

Berryman
whose elegy you hoped to avoid,
Schwartz so paranoid
he couldn't sit with his back to the door,
Uncle Devereux,
your usable grief
doled out in flickering prose in your final poems,
drunken scholar,
insatiable ego,
unfaithful husband,
why can't we remember you as one who suffered and wrote?

As one
who did not know you
I let you open like an ocean
on the coast of Maine,
the vertigo of a lighthouse beam
too much to bear.

I hated your scholarly black-
rimmed glasses
advancing to the tip of your nose
as you peered down
disdainfully at another not in the photograph.
But I got over that
when I entered the labyrinth myself,
a thread
leading me back to sanity.
Or was it bread crumbs?
Either way,
I wear myself out in a world now
so bizarre
I wouldn't be surprised if you were right,
our children "exploding into dynamite."
Go forward? Or go back?
I wish for the voice of heaven,
like a psalm
so beautiful it brought us all to tears.

I know nothing of your glory.

I liked
your more than eloquent caterwaul,
your decisiveness,
articulate as that myth nightly gutted
by beak and claws,
flying in miles over the mind's
black landscape,
your punishments made public in your sonnets.

I will sing your final sonnet
you called "Obit"
as if it were inspired by an angel
down from God,
"earth's fairer children" everywhere
though you are gone,
with grace,
given over to cruelty of time and ruin.

When My Son Comes Up from Helping
with My Neighbor's Horses

he asks
why I threw the kitten over the fence
next to the mailbox, and I tell him I had to,
it didn't understand
we couldn't keep it,
prying it from Colleen's white blouse

where it clung, without crying,
wanting to follow us

up to the house. *Here*,
I say, handing him the flashlight,
*go out to the shed and check
the water level*, and he leaves,
not quite satisfied
with what I've said. I sit

in the living room while everybody
gets into bed, regretting

my decision,
brooding unusually long for me
who flung a pillow case of mewling kittens
into my uncle's pond
one summer, wincing
when he slapped me on the back.

I slid beneath his hand,
not because I'd done

what I didn't understand
only that he did not pity me
for killing at command. Sleep

breathes evenly now
where my son lies
in the nearby light of the kitchen.

I lift my hand to his stillness, stopping
to see if he wakes
without light
on his eyelids. He sleeps on and on,
already grown passed the time
when I would lift him
from the couch
and set him down gently on his bed.

His face is Christ-like when Christ
was only a child,

not sure of what
he'd suffer, cared for by parents
who would keep him from being harmed,
flailing if they knew
how brutal
the truth would be twenty years down the line.

Human Fallibility

The monarch butterfly has flown in
from a long way off

to bask on the blossom of daisy fleabane
this dawn, this day

I will remember for the monarch butterfly
drifting and alone

throughout the shade and sunlight of October.
Now, with one flutter,

I see the brilliant brown and orange butterfly
shift a little

so suddenly she is looking up
from under a cluster

of blossoms.

Who really cares what the butterfly
claims as her own

other than these perfectly irrelevant blossoms
and her lover,

so bitter about the adoration
she lavishes on a world of flowers and yellowing leaves?

Her lover is gone
in an arc over the drift of the pines.

Suddenly, she flutters
to another, grateful for her radiance in the radiance of dawn,

spreading her great golden wings
to dry.

Years

Here, in the perfect serenity
of the golf course I rode with my father as a child,
the sheer fall of the cart onto the fairway
after the white speck lifted high
off to the right, the ascent to the green
on the only hole my father lost three balls
curving far into the cottonwoods beyond the pond . . .
the call of the distant voice
coming from somebody behind
who seemed to be asking *more* from the world
while we winced and looked wildly up . . .
the silence of my father relighting his pipe
after the par on number seven, sitting
with me overlooking the green world,
I remember the strangers that played through
dressed in slacks, and the confusion
as to whose ball was whose, the man who cursed
and cast an embarrassed glance
while we waited for him to be far enough away,
the calm of the greens in an enclosure
of sycamores and ash and the apprehension,
I remember the rage that made my father
flail at nothing in the air, losing his balance,
the shyness when he hit the perfect drive
so long and true it seemed to vanish . . .
The love of perfection
and the disgust . . .
divinity driving the ball beyond the rough,
rain on the final hole,
my father's familiarity with the other men
in the clubhouse, the taste of Hamm's.
He called me by name when we were there
as though I were one of them
and knew how to move with assurance in that world.
And I remember the Titleist I searched for

sliced clear of the water hazard.
It was twilight and I surprised
a pheasant through a maze of branches
raining down leaves, a violent fluttering.
I was so frightened I started to run,
cutting my thighs on thorns of the wild rose
before arriving along the shore
of a river where four gulls separated into pairs.
Elated to be alone, I heard my father
calling as though from the other side of life.
But I loved the river at evening and at dawn.
And then there was the long climb to the Dodge
and my father's compliance when I asked to steer
from the parking lot,
serenity of the lawns already fading
from memory while I drove
through miles of night without even smiling,
the mirror in the windshield set
against the stare from my father's brown eyes.

At the Back of the Funeral Cortege

We can see
the cortege coming from a long way off,
led by a light
spinning in the distance,
and pull our cars
over to the side of the highway
as it passes
slowly over the thin strip of asphalt,
the hearse, first,
curtained,
perhaps the immediate family
in the back seat
of a Buick, newly waxed and white,
and then
all of the tearless mourners gliding behind,
one girl
cheerless beside the window and peering
around the ear
of her father, relaxed, one hand on the wheel.
Is this
the procession we remember best
because we see
ourselves in the limousine without any needs?
I check
my wristwatch and guess
the last,
then press my foot on the pedal,
fighting
my desire to turn back and follow
the line of cars
entering the intersection
where, astride
their motorcycles sending out silver light,

two cops
hold out their palms to an uncomprehending car,
which stops,
and they take off their helmets to the dead.

III

Father

My father hated tomatoes and only swore once,
when I touched his upright sole above the covers.
It was the love of a child, without thought,
that blew a stupendous bubble over his head
one summer and watched it wobble and slide,
slicker than a womb, till he reached up
and pressed it with his forefinger and thumb.
Thirty years have passed since that bubble popped.

If time exists at all it exists in the mind
of an angel so degraded she could bathe for days
without being clean, without being cauterized. I'd like to find
my father again and say that simple name
that signifies obedience to someone wiser.
"Father," I would say, not to apologize,
"do you remember the time . . . " and he would nod,
remembering every trick I pulled as a child.

If My Friend Were in Heaven

for Larry Moffi

Taking the field
for the first time since
you hit my easy pitch
deep into the bleachers,

I imagine you have more
on your mind than pleasing
the coach, barely visible
within the dugout and shouting
to play further back
than was your habit,

spearing the line drive
curving into your glove
and whipping it to second.
Now you are an apparition
chasing the ball back
to the warning track and
catching it over your shoulder
and nothing gets by,

not even the high fly ball
that has you leaning
backwards into the stands,
touched by your admirers.
Ninth inning. Nobody out.
A man on second and the lights
illuminating you in right,
spitting into your glove.
How does that sound?

What's glory but a chance
to redeem yourself for fumbling

something in a former life?
Get ready. You will take
the scudding ball directly
in front of you without
looking up at the runner
rounding third, and throw
in mid-stride with all
your might, remembering
nothing of the time you loafed
with the game on the line
toward the clean single
and opening your glove
felt fear at its veering,
too late to salvage
your mistake
and you let the ball get by.

The Vigil

After the bath
I let the water out and draw
another for my son,
sitting like a buddha with his book
in the living room,
his mustard-stained long underwear
up to his knees,
not even seeing me when I cast my shadow
over his lap,
saying, *Go take a bath*,
which he does,
still reading as he rises.
I let the flames
in the fire-place go out
and, resisting sleep,
read of a mother in *The Tuscaloosa News*
who watched
her daughter slip through ice,
not even screaming,
then tried to die by swallowing lye
days later,
blamed for letting her get away.
When I
look up my wife is telling me to sleep.
It's then
I realize my son is not in bed,
he's gone
unless he lingers in the bathroom with the light
still on
glowing below the door
I open
to a thick mist . . . . I see him
sleeping,
his mouth just out of the water.
His eye-

lids twitch and his chest
rises, falls,
so I know he is only dozing,
the bar
of Ivory hovering beside him.
For a second
I bend
over the edge of the tub
and touch
him once, on the forehead,
but he
is much too deep to feel my finger.
How thin
and unbelievably pale
he seems,
his legs sprawled and his genitals
scarcely there,
hairless and flaccid and vaguely
swaying
in the bath, lukewarm now,
his palms
spread out on the perfect surface.
I wait
for him to stir, staring at his face,
and say
to myself, softly,
that I may
or may not go on standing here
until his eyes
are opened and he knows . . .
knows what?
That not only Dante
lost
his way in a chorus of human screams
and had
to be redeemed. That I knew
a man
who never looked lovingly at his wife

more than twice,
chasing her with a butcher knife
and holding
her down and saying, "The only person
meaner
than me is the devil."
That this world
we live in, however briefly, for better
or worse,
is where the loving mother
comes to grief
below what Shakespeare called *deaf heaven*
and dies
before the heart can comprehend
the loss
hating the God that made her.
All this, for instance,
until he lifts
his dripping
arms and whimperingly pleads
for me,
holding out his hand.
Then, perhaps,
I will take him in a towel
and turn
him around, drying his hair,
and send
him off to bed without a kiss.
Till then,
I say *Take heart*,
even in
so strange a place as this.
I keep
my vigil and refuse to move.

Past the Remaining Animals

The animals do not want us,
flying or pacing or just at rest.
Why does the gorilla
vomit into its palm,
the monkey grab its cock?
Only the gazelle is still,
a study in apprehension.
Shame on the lions
shitting in front of women,
and languid bear
licking a pallid loin.
Shame on the baboon
that peeks at its hands
like a human being and screams.
I want the dangerous dream
of a leopard in the dark
and escape of zebra,
not dung
in the dungeon of rhinoceros
and hippo. Then
I come into a silent room
where the spectator
does not speak,
seeing the slow cobra
coil and uncoil
until it is comfortable.
And I remember every
curve, every crevice,
along that monastery floor
closing my eyes,
opening them to the cobra
alone in another corner,

and clairvoyant.
This is the horror
we have been waiting for
and take with us
past the remaining animals.

An Actual Wife

The hermit has trampled a path
through old apple trees leading into the valley,
   ripping the vines and hacking
the branches down. And now at twilight
   we can see the ancient glow
of his light below the mountain, a flicker,
   otherwise lost in haze,
ribbons of chimney smoke lifted high, spiralling,
   diminishing in the wind
of late October. Where does he get
   his sustenance? Why has he sequestered himself
down there? Standing on a rock
   offering a view
of this valley, we can imagine the hermit
   hauling wood, watched by his dog.
Did we hear the echo of an ax as we climbed the path
   curving into the valley?
The surrounding pines, each of which knows
   the hermit's face
by heart, utter a cry we identify as the whipporwill,
   giving this scene
a grandeur that transcends the ordinary
   landscape, captured
in photographs. We can see the river
   at this distance,
a silver crease, beautiful only to the true outsider.
   Sunlight still shines
on the opposite side of the valley, solemnly
   turned toward the hermit
speaking before he spits into his fire.
   Does he have any faith
that he will change someday? No longer diffident?
   No longer alone?
And yet remain the same? Does he wonder
   if he's being watched by us?

And if he knew that we were talking here,
    would he circle back,
confronting us with his gun, his curiosity satisfied
    at last? What would he do
if we darkened his doorstep, peered
    into his window,
certain we were seeking an illusion from above the valley?
    Surely he would ask us
in, embarrassed by the scarcity of chairs.
    Surely he would explain
why he came to live here in the valley,
    clearing a path
opening out over the highway above our house.
    Perhaps he actually has
an actual wife, slender and serene,
    reading before the fire
while he sleeps tonight, turning the pages slowly
    as though the lines
were to be savored at the bottom
    of each page, closing
that book only when hope for the heroine
    has been revived. Suppose
she never left him
    fraught with incredible longing.
Why does he leave his light on for so long?
    What does he do all night?
Does he have a donkey? A guitar?
    Meanwhile, we linger
here, reluctant to let go of our view
    of the valley
we cannot imagine without the hermit,
    habitually grim,
gazing up at us from far below.

Remembering Death

Each day, darkness below the elms,
    light everywhere else,
  I pass the cemetery,
getting only a glimpse of the many headstones

as I drive by in my Pontiac, the traffic
    light on the highway
  and my eye
wavering between that solitude of grass

and the white line. No wonder
    so many deaths
  occur along this stretch,
bright crosses hammered into the hillside

to horrify the beholder coming and going,
    a quick death,
  the driver thrown,
while the dead let out a cry at the grinding

of steel on steel, indifferent to the passerby
    who tries to flag
  another driver down
and is met with a whoosh and silence.

Coming upon a cemetery in an open field
    I saw so many blackbirds
  their wingbeats left me
bending into evergreens. I know it is hopeless

to meditate on the dead, yet I wonder
    at their serenity
  and the silence: green canopies,
the casket shines, silence after the final shovel-full is cast.

Should I have had Isiah's vision
    or been blinded
  on the road to Tuscaloosa once
like Paul: God the only cure for my hypochondria?

Eight years ago today I woke beside my wife
    and wrote in my notebook
  a list of Do's
and Don'ts. Don't blame the world for anything

you didn't get. Don't drink alone.
    And visit a cemetery
  now and then. *Memento mori.* The latter
has kept me busy and I bear no grudge against the world

even as I see today cars hurrying to get
    through the light.
  "Slow down," the reticent dead
might say, "and live." Why then do I accelerate

mindlessly past McFarland Mall, going around sleek cars,
    Cameros, Grand Torinos,
  Sierra Classics—past the church
muted on Mondays, a row of brownstone houses?

The cars rush on, blinkers indicating right,
    not left, into the suburbs
  where everybody comes
to rest, in sleep-light, breathing throughout the night.

Mercy for a Girl Turned Over to Face the World

"Hast thou faith?
Have it to thyself before God."
                                    —St. Paul

I know what to do
when the only book consoling me
has the master saying
the silence of these infinite spaces frightens me.
I step out of the house,
breathe, seeing
the sleeping neighborhood go on sleeping.
Slight wind, blowing
the odor of cattle into town,
carries no word of what is hoped to be.
I know enough to leave such lines,
leaning out over the porch,
putting my hand around a blossom
closed golden and very cold.
I feel the impurity of another world.
Why do I
like this silence and those lights?
I see the evening star in the maple tree
past highway 85 and beyond.
A single steeple there.
The sickle moon and several stars
are far away. No pity in their glimmering.
Yet they are beautiful
scattering light against a background
near dawn. I don't know why
light means more to me than it did.
It does. The moon,
dragging its rag of darkness across the sky,
stays with me now. What can you do?
I remember fire on a night like this
cornering a woman, waving out the window,

a blaze, brilliant to the disinterested eye,
that burned against the faces of spectators
turning to confide. I could see her
lasting in the hands of her father
only a moment,
the father sobbing long as the fire survived
well into the night. I knew that man,
never the same as when he raked and laughed,
lofting a can of Schlitz
then catching it, not spilling a drop. He would
not speak after that, averting his eyes.
What accounts for man's curiosity for fire?
Burning a wind-swept field,
or flickering back and forth on a candle
carried down a hallway in the dark
as if it were unholy, that flame
wakes in me a life
that will not be fulfilled,
an interlude lingering in the mind.
I have learned to listen
for the call that comes.
I put my pencil down.
I prepare my hands.
What are the possibilities
given the inspiration to create a place,
time, and human touch?
Here where the yellow petal
reclines on my palm, a prelude,
I see a beetle
creeping in its sleep across a landscape
that is vast, answering to no one.
No more perplexities at forty,
Confucius said, wise
beyond the wisdom of women and men.
The slow breeze of the breath
of a God, too far away to be rebuked,
sweeps the trees,
influenced by movement of wind in the upper branches.

I open my hands,
noticing sunlight, colder and more remote,
and this hour leaning through evergreens
resembles the illumination Dante saw
walking out of hell, into the assurances
of the comedy. I try
to visualize those fires
flickering along the bottom, Dante gawking, heaven
just the descent of leaves for me,
only a breeze
to shake them loose. God,
gravely ill and given to lapses of silence
will not rise
as we would like – the flight of a moth
across the lawn. Yet I am consoled
knowing how slowly others discovered
we must be ready
to leave the earth at a moment's notice,
frightened by the mind's
argument with the heart.
Have you any doubt hell is here?
The heart says *yes*.
The mind insists it isn't true,
raging, a fire surprising me
at 5 A.M. that will
not be put out, even though I close
fingers around a blossom,
focusing on growing sunlight.

This is the hour
in which the patient either lives or dies.
Two brothers lit a match and blew
a moment late to live through childhood,
fumes igniting a plume
visible to their mother pumping water
into her daughter's hands, at the edge of town.
In that hour they were lifted
and borne by ambulance, on their backs,

three days away from the grave
and able to make light
of each other's strangeness
on stretchers, the youngest brother:
Larry, you look awful,
to which the other, gazing sideways,
said, *You look simply beautiful,*
and died in the highest room
the mother pumping water into her daughter's hand
could see at night
if she had looked up
pausing to rub the ache from her arms
and hands. When the wind
comes up in summer, lifting dust in a whirlwind,
I look for a woman made by the imagination
of a saint, Dante,
sketching with the pen before it strays
into the ancient story,
structured to approximate a life's
search downward, everywhere the patience of an angel.
I watch that whirl wear down the prairie
till it's a wisp, spewing a vivid blossom
across the sky, wishing my sympathy
went with Paolo and Francesca.
My sympathy is with the dust,
driven by wind that won't relent,
created by Alighieri
filled with fear, when he perceives the lovers.
Out in the dark I dream a woman
desperate to get away. The paramedics wrestle
with that death, the horror before their eyes.
Why try so hard to bring her back to life?
What I am trying to find for you
now is forgiveness,
a murderer, taking pains
to contrive the death of his mistress
night after night, using arsenic, using his fists,
who turned to his wife

at dawn before he died, by injection,
sitting with bitterness in her eyes
and said, *I have no hatred
in my heart. I have to ask you to forgive me.*
Forgiveness for the life.
Sleep, that is what my father sought
after fire embraced him.
He slept through his convalescence.
I hear him screaming when I see
a match with the ambition of a bonfire,
too late to smother the exonerating flames.
Why should there be anything other than nothing?
Why are we here? What is it like to die?
Only the blossom, whose bloom is brief,
knows the appropriate silence,
opening so slowly as to confuse
even further. In the blue dawn in the cold,
the souls of the unborn rise.
This is not a vision.
Folding my hands, I find I have been speaking
to myself. The souls
of the unborn know what I say.
They have already heard this story,
secrets I keep from myself
I can't stop telling others.

Before the Movie Begins

The light is dimmed and something like love
comes over every one of us, the kids
off to my right calming to a whisper and a couple
close to death (they must be in their eighties)
helping each other with their coats,
then sitting silently before the movie begins;
but there is awhile still for light
conversation and even mild applause
when a can is kicked over and descends
this hillside of cement facing the screen;
time for the late-comers that flood the seats
with light near the door to stumble one
behind the other down the aisle
and the attendant to reprimand a teenager
for shrieking, steering his beam of light in her eyes.

See how the arm is lifted at last
alongside the neck of another,
how the head of a woman leans
and the failures of everyone are forgiven
with a hand that caresses the hair of a man
unhappy with his life; a family
passes popcorn back and forth
while somebody shows a wristwatch
to the screen to see how much time we have.
There is the girlfriend glad for the first time
since the dance, when the one
around whom she has constructed her future
fell into the arms of the first-to-ask;
there are the brother and sister in the front
dropped off by their parents and scarcely visible.

What is this sudden kinship that I feel
with the people in this half-empty theatre,
not only the old couple closing

the wrapper on their candy so they won't be tempted,
the children too, and horde of adolescents
grooming themselves in the darkness
that diminishes the longer we all sit here?
Who will be the martyr? Who will grieve?
Who will discover love at the end of a long
and mystifying life and die in peace?
Somebody changes seats and their fate
is altered . . . or they remain the same;
the curtain parts and we prepare
(a child touched to silence, an anonymous *shissh*)
for what is coming, and does not come.
And we see each other completely in the light.

IV

Looking at the Elephant over My Shoulder

Just another June day and then an elephant
appears through the windshield of my car. How strange,
how absolutely marvelous
this huge sauntering hump being led around a ring
on the lawn of Jack's fast-food restaurant
for promotional purposes no doubt,
although what possible analogy could there be
with an elephant wrapped in a blanket
that says ELMO in large white letters?

I arrive in the almost religious
ecstasy of being in the presence of an elephant,
fathers coaxing shy daughters into the care
of the handler who ushers them up the movable stairs
and, with gentleness, lifts and sets them down
on the broad back. This is happiness
for even those on the highway,
their faces struck with wonder . . .

   One night, in bed,
borne aloft in dreams and feeling
     just elation
    (I was getting away from my ex-wife)
   I woke to a woman
        all in white

below the ceiling, shimmering
in candle-light. "From heaven, as you name it
    (we have no designation), I've been asked
to appear.
     So here I am.
Is this sufficient for you to change your ways?"

"Beatrice," I cried.

"No, Doris, done with living.
I will not haunt you with the truth
  but only say
you got it wrong. Patience is the way."

    Was she
    the angel that fought so long
  with Jacob?

          An elephant
so tolerant of strangers, so morose,
rocking primordial as the ocean.
I have to suppress my impulse to pay whatever it is worth
to feel the backbone of a god walking
between my thighs. After rides
the introspective elephant turns away
his baleful head, tugging at the rope,
hind leg lifted slightly, and he seems
on the verge of sleep. What must he think?
Does he dismiss his suffering
with, *Forgive them, they know not what they do?*

  When she had gone, I lay
    my head
on the pillow, chalking it up to booze,
    determined
  to stay off liquor for a while.

Out of nowhere, again she came, enraged.
    "Death will be miserable.
  You ought to be afraid."

  Praying throughout the night, next to my bed
    she stayed.
I joined her in my pyjamas.

A child, close to slipping, her eyes wide, clutches the tough hide.
The sun is low

over the treeline, cars come from the dramatic show of love
for the one who says nothing at all,
who does as he is told
with the flick of a stick against his quivering flank.

Another child, nearly toppled by shifting shoulder-bones,
shrieks and clings to the delicate scarf of hair
as Elmo pauses—indifferent to the awe of everyone.

> *At dawn,*
> *she fled. I saw this spirit rising in the air.*
> *She said, "Go back*
> *to the daffodil you spotted on the path,*
> *breathe deeply,*
> *enough to catch the scent.*
> *Look into the heavens. Aren't they frightening?"*

"Don't get too close,"
a mother warns, then glides her palm along him
as he passes. No one notices. I stare,
then steer apart, looking at the elephant over my shoulder.

Need

"Mercy has many arms."
     —Roethke

I watched two women make love once
when I lived in Iowa City
and the wind and snow blew
in January like the absence of mercy.
While two women I knew embraced
on a mattress
in candle-light flowering above their heads,
I stood outside a window
with the uneasiness of man about to take a vow,
my hands in my pockets,
glancing around
into a world without any innocence,
the brunette whose sweetness I had tasted
looking through her long legs
while her lover drank deeply
spreading the thighs wider by pressing gently
with her open hands,
the woman I had come to love letting her face
fall away so her hair
pooled on the floor and her tongue
licked over her lips
and she lay with her palms up
and arched her back,
saying something I could not hear
from my sanctuary of wind,
a phrase that might have forever changed me.
I watched, closer to the pane
scarred by ice
that let me see
until euphoria shook Elizabeth loose
and they lay apart
in the flow of the candles,

too sated to move. I believe they might have seen me
if I had blinked,
since both with half-closed eyes gazed out into the night.
When the light from the house behind me
shed its vastness over the snow
I vanished
through bare branches leaving tracks
they would find later
when a neighbor pointed out
the need to be more careful,
to draw the blinds and never go out alone.
I believe they would have named me
with a sickening hiss,
allowing me to flee like cellophane blown wildly
across the street,
reconsidering every kindness used to define men.
And I think they would have crucified me
with silence
and I would have had to justify my eyes
to Elizabeth who had softly touched my face.

All I could think of was that negligee
lifted over the breasts
and legs that did not resist the parting hands,
all I wanted to recall
was the tongue feasting on flesh so pure
it was appalling.
Lying awake that night in my apartment
I whispered to the stranger I had created,
who called on me
to go back over every moment of what I saw.
I knew what I was doing
when they worried over foot-prints the following day
and image of a hand
on the window where I fed my emptiness,
afraid of being caught.
I gave in easily,
not knowing if the shudder that swept over me

was inspired by wind
or desire
so deep I could have cried out,
crashing my fist through the window
as they slid from the scent
of the bed
to the hardwood floor and fumblingly rose,
touching
each other with a tenderness reserved for strangers.

I told no one what I saw.

In February
with wind blistering my face and my fingers aching
I came to a church
named after an angel and waited wildly in the nave,
watching the flames
of the candelabra accentuate the craving
of one about to suffocate, his eyes
shut down as if ashamed,
so emaciated
I thought I heard the outcry of his bones
beginning to break
and I escaped
before the priest put something on my tongue.

Now, nearing my house that can't be seen
from the highway, I notice
the leaves of the hickory beginning to change.
It is dark in the living room and all I see
is my daughter's aquarium through the door,
fish I watch when I am tired,
black mollies, angelfish
lifting their long fins in the heated water.

I should remember them for their sensual
choreography.

How considerate they are
of one another's need to drift
without interference,
not even flinching when I press
my hand to the glass,
lightly rising and gliding off to the side.

After Mass

Going home I notice in the cemetery glow
an enormous crow opening wings
on the forehead of Jesus as he pleaded
for some way out of this. "For God's
sake, Dennis, do you have to be so morbid?"
my wife inquires, craning to see
claws embracing the face in supplication.
"It just looked so unusual to me."
The dogwood blossom is taken
as a symbol for the cross; it is said
that when you hold it open on your palm
you can see the moment of apostasy.
It was the beginning of spring
and Jesus, passionate and rational
as that look lovingly cast upon the self,
asked, "What will become of me?"
the angel descending softly
to wait in human silence by his side.
Lifted alluringly above the trees,
the moon appeared through moving clouds.
Wind drew through the trees
and it was apparent that the man
understood at last the silence we accept
as final. Not far away
Peter woke from his ignorant sleep
and going no further than the olive tree
asked what my son asked just
the other day, "What can I say that you might listen to?"
I recall the instant almost blissfully:
Judas drew his cloak
over the shoulder of Jesus
and offered his lips
to the one who refused to turn
his face away—brief
but lasting eternally, this kiss,

alarmingly quick,
the length of an outstretched
arm from me. I too
have courted the confidence of God.
Hovering on the fringe,
I would have been chased away, a liar,
entering the procession
culminating with the crucifixion by Giotto
on my desk. I remember
wading out into the river on a dare one day
when the frisbee, flung
by a friend, flew low
over the surface and curved upward.
There was a moment when my light
feet lifted off the bottom
and I felt taken. I turned
my eyes to the one who dared me,
knowing the horror of my mistake.
Did the betrayer
in Gesthemane
see the tired Messiah
walk off in a throng of bearded unbelievers,
their eyes so cold and unashamed?
Judas. There is a center
in everyone of us that won't consent to sin:
in my mind I follow him
beyond the perimeter of the city
as if I were a friend
afraid to let him out of my sight,
through cypresses pointing
to the sky at dawn,
half-gallons of milk and wrappers
on the desiccated hillside
outside town. Clutching his robe to keep
from stumbling, he crosses
the highway and hesitates
in the fumes of the diesel trucks
where I catch up with him,

exhausted, putting my arm around him
and pulling him close. Or maybe
I am mistaken and let him escape.
I have tried to say this without betraying.
Someday I will touch my lips to the font
filing out of church
and feel the chill.
I will look up and discover him
in the tree outside the Holiday Inn.
I'll say his name. Judas. And they will think I'm crazy.

Thursday night,
and I am trying the patience
of my wife who wants to know
why I am slow in deciding whether I
will stay or go to Mass tonight.
I'd rather sleep. I'd rather slip outside
to my study in the night
with fragrance of honeysuckle everywhere.
An affair is suspected between the visiting priest
and somebody who has sought his consolation.
I am not pleased. Now I see
the vivid stain of wine on his vestments
and question the psychology of the redeemer
coming closer to me. Certainly,
I am frightened by the life after death.
I could listen
all night long to learn of the peace
that passes understanding, my wife
behind the pompous baritone
who sings of love
and perpetuity to the dutiful people,
my daughter clearing her throat and joining
in after the cesura, casting furtive glances
at the priest starting to stand.
The startling serenity of the soprano
alone with her lovely voice before the congregation
comforts me, and I feel the solo

closing my eyes. Is this
what Augustine felt on the balcony
overlooking the garden at Ostia? I hold out hope
I will find the purity by simply opening my eyes.

If I know nothing beneath the sky
here is the bread, the wine,
metaphors for the life,
the crucifix shimmering in my hand.
What alternative do I have
other than to praise this vision
that will change the way I see
when I walk out tonight under the neighboring maples
and witness Him in the leaves?

The Commandment

Sometimes driving home from the library at night
I take the long way leading out of town

past Buttermilk road and the paper mill
where there is one light on and the nightwatchman

between rounds stares through a golden cubicle,
his back to the moon rising on summer nights

so he can see each vehicle on the highway. On evenings
when the stock-car races let out and a stream of lights

can be seen for over a mile, he must go crazy hoping
one will turn at the gate and girls emerge

insolently waving and flaunting their slender beauty
in the headlight's glare, perhaps a can of beer

flung end over end at him from the driver's side
as they screech away and he diligently records

this incident without criticizing the world.
In the distance the paper mill is witless

except for a single beam above us all
meant to warn the pilot flying too low

that death is a phallus of mortar and stone
and he lifts his plane heavenward with the slightest

touch of his hand and is transcendent. At such times,
easing my foot off the pedal I imagine

the suicide under my care at Mayflower Apartments
over a decade ago, when I would rise hourly from my desk

and withdraw the flashlight, flicking it on and off
to see if it still shone before descending

into the underground garage of gorgeous Camaros
and Porches, cold to the touch after midnight and abiding

side by side, which I peered into with my light
leading the way. After so many years

I admit my guilt for sometimes stopping
at the door to merely observe and going no further,

driven back by the chill and odor of gasoline.
I cannot align myself with Cain anymore and say

in response to a curious God, "Am I my brother's keeper?"
I was naive, believing the imagination placed

me above blame and bitterness borne of living
in a universe indifferent to this, someone I never knew

cramming a towel into the exhaust pipe of his Ferrari
and waiting for death to appear, a drowsiness

making it hard to lift a hand against the killer.
Those who spoke of him later knew that he

was doomed and had tried to soothe him.
I would have told him the truth and excluded

nothing, alluding to the story of a man
who left his wife and child alone one night

in a rage over potatoes cooked too long
only to come home the following dawn to find

them dead, the daughter face down in the bath
while overhead her mother swung from side

to side as though blown by wind as listless
as a summer breeze, and lifting her

learned he did not want to live with the guilt,
putting a pistol to his head and nearly

squeezing the trigger when he heard a voice
opening into what I can't describe

commanding *Don't* and he indignantly complied.
Would he have accused me of imposing my precious ego

upon the poem, declaring himself alone
with the love of death? But I did not know him.

And so I sat at my desk that night in the lobby
revising, cutting line after line until the sentiment

of endless love had been ground down to a stanza
even I did not believe, while you leaned back and breathed

deeply and were eager for life to be over
and death to begin. That did not happen.

I let the hour pass and the hour after that,
crafting the stanza and noting my supposed vigilance

over the parking lot outside the garage
you stumbled from when your gauge lay on empty.

I did not see you until the three policemen
burst through bearing a folded stretcher,

"There's been an attempted suicide in 322,"
and moved away and were surprisingly cool

at the elevator door, letting the paramedics enter
with a wave of their hand and they ascended together.

I remember and choose to forget the attempt
at suicide that lay open the tender flesh

of your wrists and splashed your bathroom
with a stain your roommate couldn't scrub away

for days, a death that fought fiercely
as Jacob in the grip of a tireless angel

and then relented when you were raised
onto the stretcher and carried quickly away

complaining the paramedics were not gentle,
the front doors opening to an ambulance

frantic with light. I remember and I lied.
Why not corroborate my story by pointing

at the page that signified the hour and my rounds?
But sometimes driving home at night

I see the nightmare again and believe everything
is possible, self-sacrifice and brotherly love and death

with more dignity than a speechless shape on the bed.
I cannot bring you back yet resurrect you

in memory passing the paper mill tonight,
maybe to explain why the imagination

lies dormant until the fear of death comes clear
to the human being, or until the love of one

becomes the love of others so completely
we forget why we were ever enamored of ourselves.

Addendum

When I was a child my father took me to the hospital
across town, telling me all I needed to know
about the dying, that they don't often comprehend
who we are, why they suffer—waiting to cross over to God.
I thought of grandfather on the edge of his bed
with his pipe put away in his coat pocket,
watching *As The World Turns* on television.
I did not want to be there when he turned completely to air,
needing no one to boil an egg anymore
or rub mentholatum on his chest. Along the way
it began to rain, and, feeling thwarted, my father
accelerated over the bridge above the Bad River.

We skidded, hitting a sign that said YIELD.

What happened after that in the ditch
is another matter, a son's ingratitude, a father's failure,
neither of whom believed a spirit's intervening
on a bridge over a river named from another century
by someone who knew the difference,
could occur in any life-time like their own.
It was hard to forgive ourselves for this.
In memory, I move in a dream
bordered by sunflowers and roses,
the beautiful sway and flow,
my father on one side and my mother on the other.
What did we know
racing down a path that is lost to us now?
And then a calm comes over us, wind cooling our faces.

Look how easily we have forgiven them all.

Dennis Sampson was born in 1949 in South Dakota and graduated from South Dakota State University where he played football and lettered in track. He received his Master of Fine Arts from the University of Iowa in 1976. His first book, *The Double Genesis*, was published in 1985 and was chosen by the NEA for display at the Frankfurt Bookfair. Poetry and criticism of his have appeared in *The Hudson Review*, *The Ohio Review*, *Crazyhorse*, and *The American Scholar*. Sampson received the Denise & Mel Cohen Award from *Ploughshares* for his poem "The Commandment." He is the recipient of an individual fellowship in creative writing from The Alabama Arts Council in 1985. Married, with three children, he lives in Tuscaloosa, Alabama and works at Shelton State Community College.